NATIONAL
GEOGRAPHIC
KiDS

# Just Joking

## SIDESPLITTERS

Rosie Gowsell Pattison

NATIONAL GEOGRAPHIC
WASHINGTON, D.C.

**300** hilarious jokes about everything, including tongue twisters, riddles, and more!

KNOCK, KNOCK.

*Who's there?*
Naan.
*Naan who?*
Naan of your business. Just open the door!

A full-grown hippo can weigh as much as three small cars.

**KNOCK, KNOCK.**

Who's there?
Cannoli.
*Cannoli who?*
I cannoli visit
for an hour.

Harp seal
mothers identify
their babies by
their smell.

**Q** What's in the middle of a jellyfish?

**A** A jellybutton.

VEGETABLE FARMER: My truck has a flat tire.

SON: How are we going to fix it?

VEGETABLE FARMER: With a-spare-I-guess.

**Q** What's **black** and **white** and **sleeps** a lot?

**A** A snoozepaper.

Say this fast three times:

**Slurp soup** on a **sloop.**

**Q** What do you call a sneaky football player?

**A** A wide deceiver.

**Q** Why wasn't the man hurt when he was hit by a soda?

**A** Because it was a soft drink.

8

The tiger quoll is a catlike marsupial found in Australia and New Guinea.

KNOCK, KNOCK.

*Who's there?*
Farmer.
*Farmer who?*
Farmer birthday, I'm going to have a chocolate cake.

9

Male elephant seals have inflatable "trunks" that they use to make loud roars to scare off other males.

## Signs you're in a bad motel:

- You have to wait for the guy next door to be done with the towel so you can use it.
- The complimentary newspaper tells you that the United States finally landed on the moon.
- The mint on the pillow runs away from you when you try to pick it up.
- There is fuzzy brown stuff on the floor, but the manager insists none of the rooms are carpeted.
- A family of cockroaches posted a negative review on the motel's website.

**MOTEL**

**POOL**

KNOCK, KNOCK.

Who's there?
Tolkien.
Tolkien who?
Last night you were Tolkien in your sleep.

Orangutans spend most of their time in trees. They will build a roof in the trees to keep dry when it rains.

**What do you call it when two pigs jump out and surprise you?**

A hambush. **A**

14

**Q** What's the difference between a **jeweler** and a **jailer?**

**A** One sells watches and the other watches cells.

**Q** Why is tennis such a loud game?

**A** Because each player raises a racket.

**Q** What do you give a rhinoceros with big feet?

**A** Lots of room.

**Q** What happens if you wear a snowsuit inside?

**A** It melts.

GROUP HUG!!!

Laugh Out LOUD

KNOCK, KNOCK.

*Who's there?*
Pun.
*Pun who?*
These jokes could use some *pun*structive criticism.

Toucans use their large bills to reach and peel fruit. They are made up of a honeycomb of bone.

18

**Q** What's a pirate's favorite movie?

**A** Booty and the Beast.

**Q** What do mermaids put on their toast?

**A** Mermalade.

19

Q What do firemen put in their soup?

A Fire crackers.

Q Where do hogs find the meaning of words?

A In the pigtionary.

Q Why did the **tap dancer quit** dancing?

A She kept falling in the sink.

Q Where did King Arthur buy exotic animals?

A At the Camel lot.

After a high-speed chase, a cheetah needs half an hour to catch its breath before it can eat its prey.

KNOCK,

KNOCK.

Who's there?
Salami.
Salami who?
Salami get this straight, you aren't ready to go yet?

21

KNOCK, KNOCK.

Who's there?
Little boy.
*Little boy who?*
Little boy who can't reach the doorbell.

Goldfish have teeth in their throats to help them crush their food.

Goats can be taught their name and to come when called.

KNOCK, KNOCK.

Who's there?
Shave.
Shave who?
Shave the jokes for later. Let's get going!

**Q** What do you call a small loaf of bread that makes a great mentor?

**A** A roll model.

**Q** Why is a jaguar so good at trivia?

**A** Because every guess is spot-on.

**Q** What do you call a grizzly in a coffee shop?

**A** A bearista.

**Q** Where did the carpenter buy his measuring stick?

**A** At a yard sale.

25

**Q**

What do you call a chef who cooks Chinese food in her sleep?

**A** A sleep wok-er.

TONGUE TWISTER!

Say this fast three times:

**The cracked crackers were kept in the cracker shack until they took their crackers back.**

**Q**

What do you get if you cross a nursery rhyme author and a citrus fruit?

**A** Mother Juice.

**Q** Where do mermaids go to watch movies?

**A** The dive-in.

A grizzly bear's bite is so powerful it can crush a bowling ball.

KNOCK, KNOCK.

Who's there?
To.
To who?
No, it's "to whom."

# Laugh Out LOUD

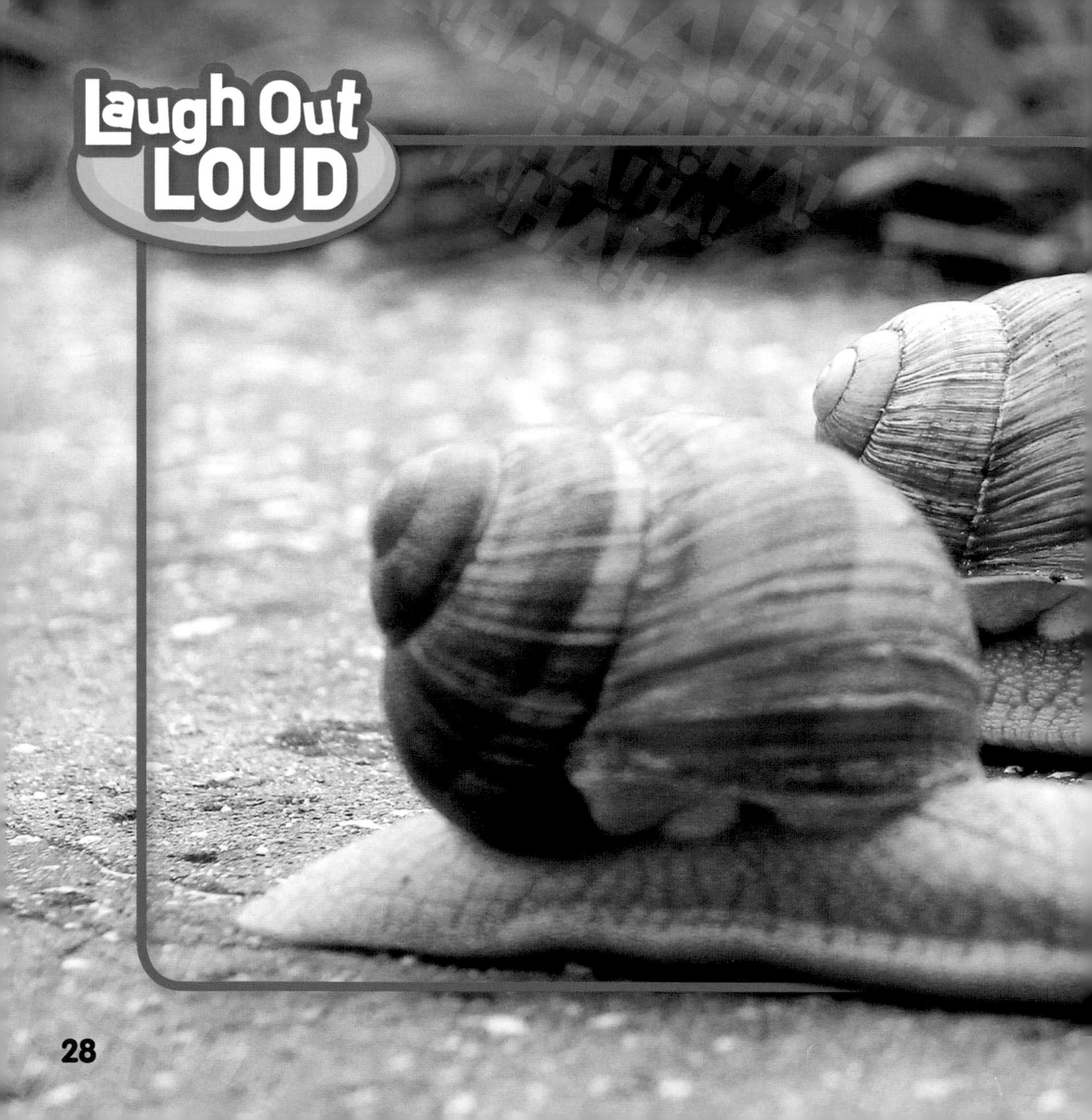

A Komodo dragon's saliva contains deadly bacteria that kills its prey, even if it escapes an attack.

KNOCK, KNOCK.

Who's there?
Minnows.
Minnows who?
Minnows is stuffy.
Got a tissue?

## Signs you have a terrible mountain climbing guide:

- He starts every day's preparation by building snow forts.
- She repeatedly asks, "Is it just me or is it chilly up here?"
- He uses the oxygen tanks to make balloon animals.
- She keeps asking if anyone is getting a cell phone signal for their GPS.
- He doesn't pack any food because he's hoping to pick up a burger along the way.

**Q** What's white, fluffy, and hangs from trees?

**A** A meringuetan.

31

**Q** What was the **pirate** **boxer's** favorite **punch?**

**A** A left hook.

**Q** What do you get when you cross a cow and a rabbit?

**A** A hare in your milk.

MILK

ONE PINT (473mL)

OPEN

**Q** Where can you **learn** all about **chickens?**

**A** In the hen-cyclopedia.

**Q** What's worse than **raining** **cats** and **dogs?**

**A** Hailing taxis.

32

KNOCK,

KNOCK.

Who's there?
Some fin.
Some fin who?
Some fin tells me this
is anofer bad knock-
knock joke.

The eyes of the celestial eye
goldfish are mounted on top
of its head and are constantly
looking upward. They are also
known as stargazers.

Water buffalo have large hoofed feet that prevent them from sinking in ponds or mud.

KNOCK, KNOCK.

Who's there?
Taurus.
Taurus who?
Niagara Falls is a popular Taurus destination.

35

36

**Q** What does an aardvark like on its pizza?

**A** Anchovies.

**Q** What kind of **beans** won't grow in your garden?

**A** Jelly beans.

**Q** Why is it hard to talk to a goat?

**A** Because they're always butting in.

**Q** What did the sink say to the water faucet?

**A** "You're a real drip."

37

**PIRATE WITH PEG LEG:** Have you been a pirate all your life?

**ONE-EYED PIRATE:** No, I used to be a teacher, but I got fired.

**PIRATE WITH PEG LEG:** Why?

**ONE-EYED PIRATE:** Because I only had one pupil.

**Q** What kind of **pie** can **fly?**

**A** A magpie.

38

A cat's tongue is covered in tiny, firm barbs called papillae. These barbs help pick dirt and debris out of their fur while grooming.

**KNOCK, KNOCK.**

*Who's there?*
Sweeter.
*Sweeter who?*
Can I borrow a sweeter? It's chilly.

**Q** Why did the ram run off the road?

**A** He didn't see the ewe-turn.

42

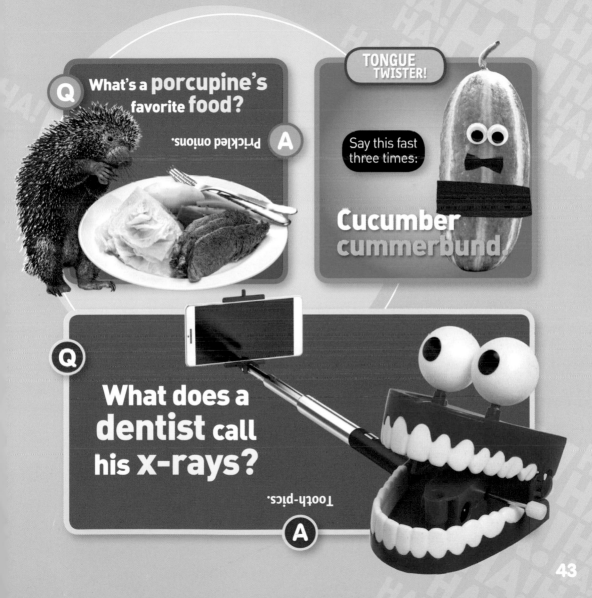

**Q** What's a **porcupine's** favorite **food?**

**A** Prickled onions.

Say this fast three times:

**Cucumber cummerbund**

**Q** What does a **dentist** call his **x-rays?**

**A** Tooth-pics.

43

KNOCK, KNOCK.

Who's there?
Goose.
Goose who?
Goose who
it is!

Goslings can swim right after hatching. They are able to fly within two months.

44

# Animal Valentine's Day cards:

- Octopus: I ink I love you.
- Deer: I'm very fawned of you.
- Dinosaur: I'm raptor round your finger.
- Wildebeest: I gnu you were the one for me.
- Snake: I hiss you were here.

**Q** What happened when the girl tried to catch fog in a jar?

**A** She mist.

45

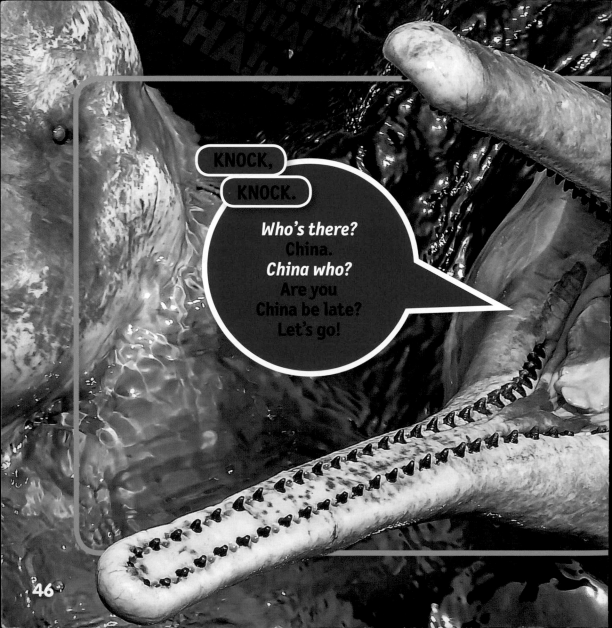

The pink river dolphin lives in the freshwater of the Amazon River. They are born gray and become more pink as they age.

**Q** Why didn't the girl get rid of her pet leech?

**A** Because she was really attached to it.

**Q** What did the **tornado** say to the **car**?

**A** "Want to go for a spin?"

**Q** Why was the vegetable soup so expensive?

**A** It had 24 karats in it.

**Q** How do you send a secret message in the forest?

**A** By moss code.

Arctic wolves have hair between the pads on their feet to keep them warm while walking on snow and ice.

**KNOCK, KNOCK.**

*Who's there?*
Paw.
*Paw who?*
You paw thing. Have you been inside all day?

**Q** Why are people in clock factories so expressive?

**A** Because they make faces all day.

**Q** What kind of **coat** goes on **wet** and **never** has **buttons?**

**A** A coat of paint.

**Q** What do you get if you cross a sheep and a porcupine?

**A** An animal that knits its own sweaters.

**Q** Where is the best place to try new bubblegum?

**A** On a chew-chew train.

NO! WE'RE WHITE WITH BLACK STRIPES!

Laugh Out LOUD

**KNOCK, KNOCK.**

*Who's there?*
Bear claws.
*Bear claws who?*
I'm knocking bear claws I want to come in!

A polar bear's paws are slightly webbed to help it swim.

54

STUDENT 1:
I'm taking French, Spanish, and Algebra this year.

STUDENT 2:
How do you say "Good evening" in Algebra?

**Q** What kind of driver never gets a speeding ticket?

**A** A screwdriver.

**Q** What is **white** when it's dirty and **black** when it's clean?

**A** A blackboard.

**Q** How do angels greet each other?

**A** They wave halo.

**Q** What do you get if you cross a snake and a kangaroo?

**A** A jump rope.

**Q** When does it **rain money?**

**A** When there's a change in the weather.

# Q

# Which flag do monkeys wave on the Fourth of July?

# A

The star-spangled banana.

Puffins are sometimes called "clowns of the sea"!

KNOCK, KNOCK.

*Who's there?*
Pasta.
*Pasta who?*
I walked right pasta house.

59

**KNOCK, KNOCK.**

*Who's there?*
Dishes.
*Dishes who?*
Dishes your mother.
Did you clean
your room?

Even though they are called black bears,
sometimes their coats can be gray or white.

**Q** Why do basketball players take so many vacations?

**A** Because they're good at traveling.

**Q** What do you get if you cross a giraffe and a rooster?

**A** An animal that wakes up people on the top floor.

Say this fast three times:

# Family financed foreign sci-fi film festival.

**Q** How do you arrest a pig?

**A** Put him in ham-cuffs.

**Q** What's green and jumpy?

**A** A grasshopper with the hiccups.

## Signs there's a hole in your pool:

- You can touch the bottom of the deep end without diving.
- Your pool "floaties" become pool "standies."
- It takes twice as long to climb out as it did when you climbed in.
- Your aqua-fit class turns into aerobics.

The darker red markings from the corner of a red panda's eyes to the corner of its mouth help to keep the sun out of its eyes.

KNOCK, KNOCK.

*Who's there?*
Nacho.
*Nacho who?*
This is nacho house! Get outta there, quick!

63

SO FAR, THESE FISH HAVEN'T FIGURED OUT WE AREN'T ONE OF THEM.

Laugh Out LOUD

The steenbok is a dwarf antelope. It has very sharp hooves it uses to dig for food.

KNOCK, KNOCK.

*Who's there?*
Corn.
*Corn who?*
Your directions to get here were very *corn*fusing.

66

**DOOR:**
Ugh, my hinges are aching!

**WINDOW:**
Stop your squeaking. I'm the one with the pane!

**Q**

What do you call a boat-shaped hat that fits your head perfectly?

Cap-sized.

**A**

67

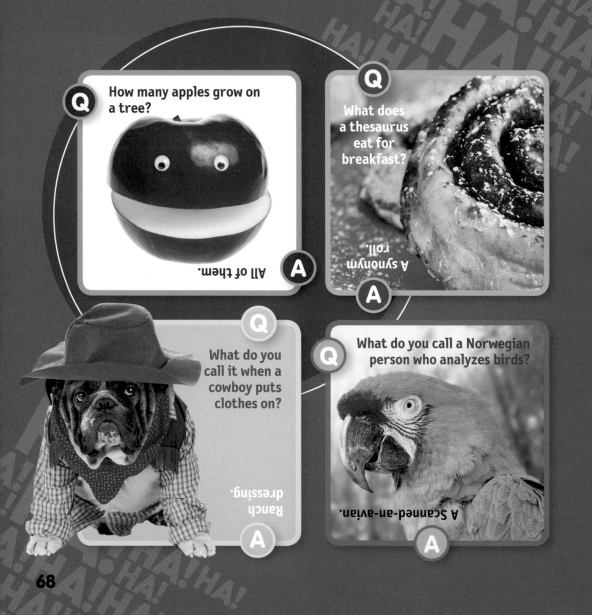

**Q** How many apples grow on a tree?

**A** All of them.

**Q** What does a thesaurus eat for breakfast?

**A** A synonym roll.

**Q** What do you call it when a cowboy puts clothes on?

**A** Ranch dressing.

**Q** What do you call a Norwegian person who analyzes birds?

**A** A Scanned-an-avian.

**Q** **Why did the gingerbread man need to see a dentist?**

**A** Because he had gingervritis.

**Q** Why do concert violinists go to the gym so much?

**A** So they can stay fit as a fiddle.

**Q** What kind of doctor prescribes soda to her patients?

**A** A pop-tometrist.

DOCTOR: You have a very contagious flu virus. We are going to have to put you in quarantine and on a special diet. You can only eat pancakes and cheese slices.

PATIENT: Pancakes and cheese slices? Will that make me feel better?

DOCTOR: No, it's the only food that we can slide under the door.

Humpback whales are known for their "singing." Their songs can travel great distances through the ocean and go on for hours.

Q

# What's long and slippery?

Size 14 slippers.

A

Q

What do you call a pie that comes back to you when you throw it?

A boomeringue.

A

Q

Why shouldn't you upset a

Because the punishment will B major.

A

Q

Which type of money weighs the most?

The British pound.

A

Who takes care of
all the **animal's teeth**
at the **zoo**?

Q

The molar bear.

A

75

Laugh Out
LOUD

Parrots are believed to be one of the most intelligent of the bird species.

KNOCK, KNOCK.
Who's there?
Hive.
Hive who?
Hive been out here for ages!

# Pig party games:

- Bobbing for Slop
- Pin the Tail on the Farmer
- Duck Duck Goose Cow Chicken Pony Goat ...
- Hogscotch

**Q** How do sweater-makers come up with new patterns?

**A** They imagine-knit.

**Q** Why did the **sick girl** go to the **shoe-maker?**

**A** So she could be heeled.

**Q** Why did the baker break up with her boyfriend?

**A** He was too kneady.

TONGUE TWISTER!

Say this fast three times:

**Brian from Britain has bitten my mitten.**

**Q** What happened when the potato chip factory caught fire?

**A** It burned to a crisp.

Tasmanian devils have muscular jaws and sharp teeth. They have one of the most powerful bites of any mammal on Earth.

KNOCK, KNOCK.

Who's there?
Pollen.
Pollen who?
Are you pollen my leg?

The hammerhead shark has a 360-degree range of vision. This means it can see in front, behind, above, and below itself at all times.

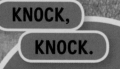

**KNOCK, KNOCK.**

Who's there?
Water.
Water who?
I just saw your friend, but I don't know water name is.

Green moray eels can grow up to eight feet (2.4 m) long.

**Q** Why did the boy who never played basketball decide to join a team?

**A** He wanted to give it a shot.

**Q** Why do **musicians** make people **laugh?**

**A** Because their jokes are pretty sharp.

**Q** Why did the hamburger go to the gym?

**A** It wanted better buns.

**Q** Why did the coffee beans go to jail?

**A** Because there were grounds for arrest.

SLOTH: Officer, I was just mugged by four snails!

OFFICER: Can you describe them?

SLOTH: I don't think so, it all happened so fast.

**Q** Why can't you trick an x-ray technician?

**A** Because they can always see through you.

KNOCK,
KNOCK.

Who's there?
Al dente.
Al dente who?
I don't want to knock
too hard. I'm afraid
al dente the door.

The word
"flamingo"
comes from
the Latin
word *flamma*,
meaning flame
or fire.

87

# How do you teach your **puppy** to **walk down** the **stairs?**

Step by step.

A

Despite having around 45 teeth, orcas can swallow small seals or sea lions whole!

**KNOCK, KNOCK.**

*Who's there?*
Swimmer.
*Swimmer who?*
Hey, swimmer down.
No need to yell.

**Q**

Why do podiatrists always make a good impression?

**A** Because they put their best foot forward.

Say this fast three times:

# Sasquatch watch shop.

**Q**

Why did the student like to take music as her last class?

**A** So she could end the day on a high note.

**Q**

What did one crow say to the other?

**A** "Give me a caw sometime."

91

**Q**

Why did the **food taster** quit his job?

**A**

Because he had too much on his plate.

**Q**

Who will fix your cavity if your dentist is on vacation?

**A**

Whoever is filling in.

**Q**

Why didn't the orchestra broadcast their concert on the internet from the tiny concert hall?

**A**

There wasn't enough bandwidth.

**Q**

## What do you call a baby monkey that's similar to its dad?

A chimp off the old block.

**A**

KNOCK,

KNOCK.

Who's there?
Shell.
Shell who?
Shell we
leave now?

94

All aboard! Tree frogs have sticky toe pads to make it easier to climb trees ... or hitch a ride.

The chameleon forest dragon is neither a chameleon nor a dragon!

KNOCK, KNOCK.

*Who's there?*
Swarm.
*Swarm who?*
Swarm today, isn't it?

**SAFARI TOURIST:** Is it hard to spot a leopard?

**SAFARI GUIDE:** No, they come that way.

**Q** What kind of animal will you find working at a print shop?

**A** Copy cats making paw prints.

**99**

**Q** Why was the dairy farmer limping?

**A** Because he sprained his calf.

**Q** What kind of insect bothers musicians?

**A** Flute flies.

**Q** Why did the banker change jobs?

**A** He lost interest.

**Q** What do you call a bee that can't make up its mind?

**A** A maybee.

Mallards can take off from water and fly almost straight up in the air.

KNOCK, KNOCK.

*Who's there?*
Bubbly.
*Bubbly who?*
I'm prob-bubbly going shopping, wanna come?

**What do you get if you cross a Halloween treat and a mythical creature?**

Uni-candy-corn.

A

**KNOCK,**

**KNOCK.**

*Who's there?*
Wool.
*Wool who?*
I wool keep knocking until you open up.

There are more than one billion sheep in the world!

104

**Q** What kind of **musicians** do you find in the **ocean?**

**A** Fiddler crabs.

**Q** Why were the towels gathered on the clothes line?

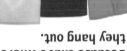

**A** Because that's where they hang out.

**Q** Why do people like fountain of youth jokes?

**A** Because they never get old.

**Q** What do you call a **test** in a **soft drink** factory?

**A** A pop quiz.

Q Why did the author write a book about his basement?

A Because he knew it would be a best cellar.

Q Why did the singer join so many singing groups?

A Because she had a-choir-ed a taste for it.

Q What do you call it when a bag of chips falls over?

A A snackcident.

Q Why did the tailor have to testify in court?

A Because he was a material witness.

Llamas will spit, hiss, or even kick when angry!

KNOCK, KNOCK.

Who's there?
Llama.
*Llama who?*
Llama take a selfie before we go.

108

**Q**

## What do you call a
## porcelain
## knight?

Sir-amic.

**A**

## Snowman illnesses:

- Frostbite
- Water on the knee
- Termites
  (affects twig
  arms only)
- A cold
- Snowflakey skin

Elephants keep cool by first spraying themselves with water and then a thin, protective layer of dust.

KNOCK, KNOCK.

*Who's there?*
Gnocchi.
*Gnocchi who?*
There's gnocchi hole in the door. How do I get in?

**Q** Which fish only comes out at night?

**A** A starfish.

**DOG 1:** Want to hear a knock-knock joke?

**DOG 2:** Sure!

**DOG 1:** Knock, kno—

**DOG 2:** BARK BARK

In India, there is a yearly festival held to "thank" cows for serving farmers.

KNOCK,
KNOCK.

Who's there?
Cud.
Cud who?
Cud you just
open the door?

113

Laugh Out LOUD

HA! HA! HA! HA! HA!
I'D BETTER GET MOVING. I DON'T WANT TO BE LATE FOR SCHOOL.

KNOCK, KNOCK.

Who's there?
Manure.
Manure who?
Manure making some awful puns today!

Pelicans use the pouch attached to their beak to scoop fish out of the water.

**Q** 3
What happened to the dog who was trespassing?

**A**
3 —
2 —
1 — He was pawsecuted.

BAD DOG
09090
POLICE DEPT.

**Q** What do you get if you cross a sheep and a landmark?

**A** The Statewe of Liberty.

**Q** What do you call a radioactive kitten?

**A** A mewtant.

RADIOACTIVE

Icelandic horses change colors with the seasons. They can be brown in the winter and gray in the spring.

The female great horned owl is larger than the male.

KNOCK, KNOCK.

*Who's there?*
Confection.
*Confection who?*
I can't get a good Wi-Fi confection out here.

**Q** How does a statue call home?

**A** On its iStone.

**Q** What do you call it when a teacher falls off a bus?

**A** A school trip.

**Q** Where does seaweed look for a job?

**A** In the kelp wanted ads.

**Q** Where do zombies like to stay on vacation?

**A** In a dead and breakfast.

123

**Q** How do birds keep their sneakers on?

**A** With velcrow.

**Q** What do you call a **magician** who's great at **trivia?**

**A** A quizzard.

**Q** What kind of photos do biologists take?

**A** Cellfies.

**Q** Which is the healthiest type of $H_2O$?

**A** Well water.

124

**Q** What do you call a **rabbit** raised in a **hotel?**

**A** An inn-grown hare.

125

Laugh Out
LOUD

The black mamba is one of the world's deadliest snakes. They are extremely venomous and very fast.

KNOCK, KNOCK.
*Who's there?*
Mint.
*Mint who?*
Come out here this very mint!

**Q** What do birds use to fix a flat tire?

**A** A crowbar.

## Fish movies:

- *The Catfish in the Hat*
- *Koi Story*
- *Walleye-E*
- *The Swordfish in the Stone*
- *Monster Tunaversity*
- *Finocchio*

**129**

**Q** What do **cat journalists report on?**

**A** Breaking mews.

**Q** What did the cell phone say to the phone charger?

**A** "I'd die without you."

**Q** What kind of dinosaur can you find on the golf course?

**A** A Tee rex.

130

KNOCK, KNOCK.

*Who's there?*
Kinder.
*Kinder who?*
I'm kinder disappointed we missed the movie.

Gulls are intelligent and mischievous birds. They play games, bother other animals, and steal prey from other birds.

131

KNOCK, KNOCK.

Who's there?
Daisy.
Daisy who?
You have a visitor?
How many daisy
staying?

Cheetahs are in danger of becoming extinct due to loss of habitat and the amount of prey available to them.

**Q**

How do birds wish each other Merry Christmas?

**A**

"Happy owlidays."

**Q**

What kind of sandwiches do they make in the ocean?

**A** Peanut butter and jellyfish.

Say this fast three times:

Seven selfish swimming shellfish.

**Q**

Who can shave 10 times a day and still have a beard?

**A** A barber.

**Q**

Why was the teenager so sad when she lost her camera phone?

**A** Because she couldn't picture herself without it.

Corgis have been part of the British royal family for more than 70 years.

136

**CUSTOMER:** How much is that duck?

**PET STORE OWNER:** Ten dollars.

**CUSTOMER:** Okay, could you please send me the bill?

**PET STORE OWNER:** I'm sorry, but you'll have to take the whole bird.

**Q**

What did the **pencil** say to the **paper**?

**A** "I dot my eye on you."

137

REPORT CARD

MATH - - - - - - - A+
ENGLISH - - - - - - B
SCIENCE - - - - - - A-
ART - - - - - - C+
MUSIC - - - - - - B+
P.E. - - - - - - A

PASS

**Q** **How was the tortoise's report card?**

Turtle-y awesome!

A

**Q** Where is a zombie's favorite place to camp?

**A** The brain forest.

**Q** What did one coffee pot say to the other?

**A** "You're brewtiful."

**Q** Why were the two bridges fighting?

**A** Because they were arch enemies.

**Q** Why did the bowl fall in love with the baker?

**A** Because it was whisked off its feet.

140

KNOCK, KNOCK.

*Who's there?*
Retriever.
*Retriever who?*
My mom went to retriever hat.

Labrador retrievers come in three colors: black, chocolate, and yellow—sometimes in the same litter!

**Q** Why don't people trust **ladders?**

**A** Because they're always up to something.

**Q** What's green and snuggly?

**A** An avocuddle.

**Q** Where does a royal mallard live?

**A** At Duckingham Palace.

**Q** Which season is the best time to trampoline?

**A** Spring time.

Why couldn't the **cephalopod focus** on its **work?**

Chacma baboons have pouches in their cheeks where they store food.

KNOCK, KNOCK.

Who's there?
Howl.
Howl who?
Howl we be able to make up lost time?

**KNOCK, KNOCK.**

*Who's there?*
Mush.
*Mush who?*
Thank you sho mush.

As baby birds grow, they are called different names: nestling, hatchling, or fledgling.

146

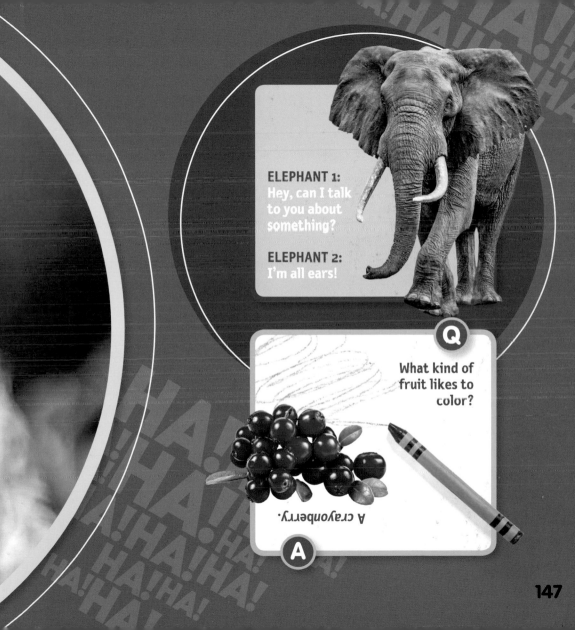

ELEPHANT 1:
Hey, can I talk to you about something?

ELEPHANT 2:
I'm all ears!

**Q** What kind of fruit likes to color?

**A** A crayonberry.

147

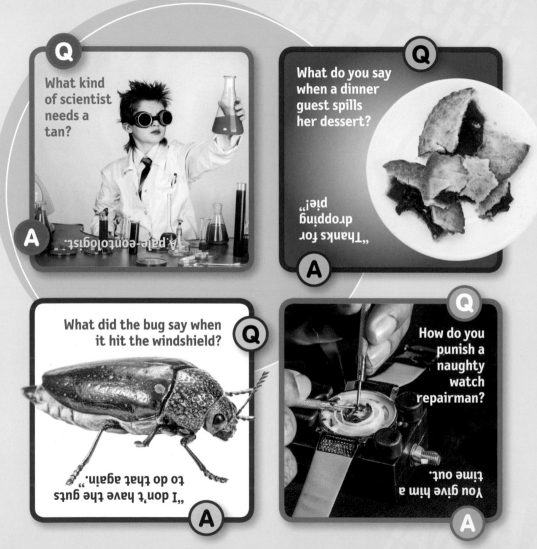

**Q** What kind of scientist needs a tan?

**A** A pale-eontologist.

**Q** What do you say when a dinner guest spills her dessert?

**A** "Thanks for dropping pie!"

**Q** What did the bug say when it hit the windshield?

**A** "I don't have the guts to do that again."

**Q** How do you punish a naughty watch repairman?

**A** You give him a time out.

148

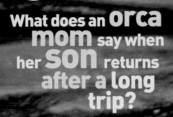

What does an **orca mom** say when her **son** returns after a long trip?

"Whalecome home, son!"

153

KNOCK, KNOCK.

Who's there?
Mastiff.
Mastiff who?
This is a mastiff
waste of time.

The bullmastiff
rarely barks
or bites.

**Q** What do you call it when a man wearing boxers is being pursued by the police?

**A** A brief chase.

**Q** What do you get if you cross a crow and a hippo?

**A** A lot of broken telephone poles.

**Q** How did the king find his lost son?

**A** He followed the foot-prince.

**Q** What does Canada produce that no other country produces?

**A** Canadians.

**Q** What did the cup and saucer think of the pot's party?

**A** It was tea-rrific!

**Q** Why was a kitten running an MRI machine?

**A** Because the doctor ordered a CAT scan.

156

**KNOCK,**

**KNOCK.**

*Who's there?*
Ivory.
*Ivory who?*
Ivory now and
then I like to
stop by.

Lionesses hunt for food
from dusk till dawn.
They do 85–90 percent
of the hunting for
the pride.

The Gila monster is one of only two known venomous lizard species.

# Laugh Out LOUD

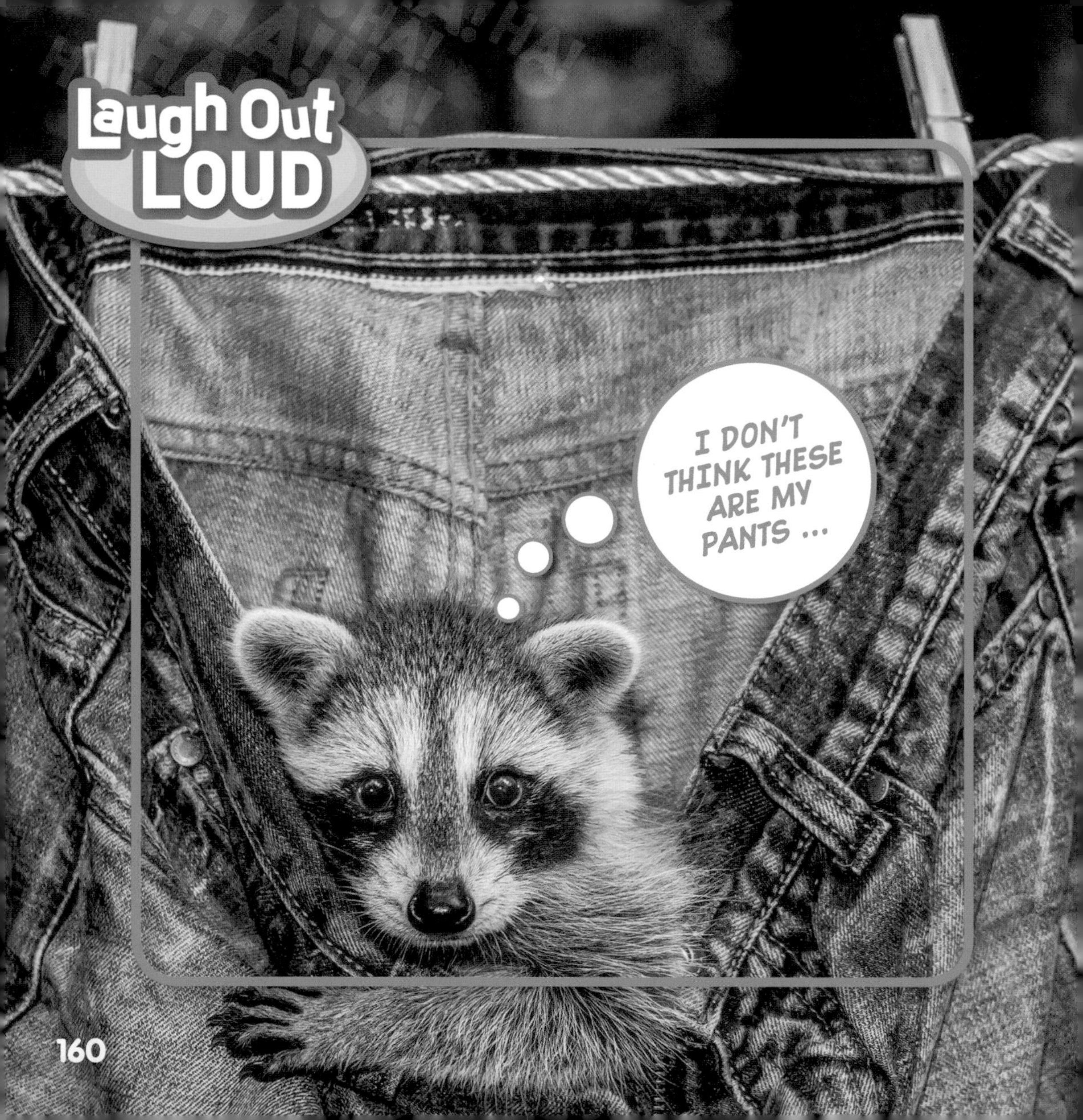

**Q** Which contest did the broom win?

**A** The sweepstakes.

**Q** Why did the kid wear two jackets while painting the fence?

**A** His dad told him to put on two coats.

**Q** Why do people whisper in the pharmacy?

**A** So they don't wake the sleeping pills.

**Q** What do aliens like to read?

**A** Comet books.

# Animal books:

- *Dairy Potter*
- *Kitty Kitty Bang Bang*
- *James and the Giant Leech*
- *Winnie-the-Moo*
- *Moby Duck*

If a Scottish terrier gets too excited, they may get a temporary "Scottie cramp" where their muscles tense up. They'll walk funny until it passes, but it doesn't hurt them.

**Q**

What does a superhero put in their iced tea?

Just-ice.

**A**

KNOCK,
KNOCK.

Who's there?
Terrier.
Terrier who?
We all make mistakes;
don't terrier self
up about it.

KNOCK, KNOCK.

*Who's there?*
Foal.
*Foal who?*
Quit foaling around
and get out here.

A horse's eyes are bigger than those of any other mammal that lives on land.

BOB: I can cut a piece of wood in half just by looking at it.

DOUG: No you can't!

BOB: It's true. I saw it with my own eyes.

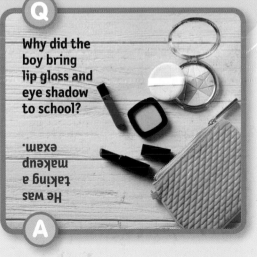

Q Why did the boy bring lip gloss and eye shadow to school?

A He was taking a makeup exam.

167

**KNOCK, KNOCK.**

*Who's there?*
Gibbon.
*Gibbon who?*
I was gibbon the wrong address.

Gibbons avoid water because they can't swim.

**Q** What kind of bugs live in clocks?

**A** Ticks.

Say this fast three times:

**Whose shoes does she choose?**

**Q** What **position** does **Bruce Wayne** play on his **baseball team?**

**A** Bat boy.

**Q** What's red and goes up and down?

**A** A tomato in an elevator.

170

**Q** What **weighs** a ton and is **really trendy?**

**A** A hipsterpotamus.

171

**Q** What did the chef give her husband for Valentine's Day?

**A** A hug and a quiche.

**Q** What's green, has eight legs, and comes with **chips**?

**A** A guactopus.

**Q** What do you get if you cross a wasp and a precious jewel?

**A** A rubee.

**Q** How do you make a cat float?

**A** Two scoops of ice cream, some root beer, and a cat!

173

**Q** Why couldn't the trout get money out of the ATM?

**A** He had insuffishent funds.

**Q** How can you tell when a doughnut is daydreaming?

**A** Its eyes are glazed over.

**Q** What's a **pirate's favorite letter?**

**A** You'd think it's r but it be the c.

I DON'T THINK THIS IS A GUMBALL ...

Laugh Out LOUD

KNOCK,
KNOCK.

*Who's there?*
Whale.
*Whale who?*
Aren't you going
to whale-come
me inside?

Baby birds are
forced to leave the
nest before they
are mature so they
can learn important
survival skills.

KNOCK,
KNOCK.

*Who's there?*
Hollandaise.
*Hollandaise who?*
There's no place
like home for
the hollandaise.

Foxes have vertical pupils, similar to those of cats. This helps them to see well at night.

MANAGER: There's a broken bottle of oil in aisle two.

EMPLOYEE: How much of it spilled?

MANAGER: Olive it.

EMPLOYEE: I canola imagine how long it will take to clean up.

**Q** What kind of music do chefs play in the kitchen?

**A** Wok-and-roll.

179

**Q**

What do you get if you cross a **kangaroo** and an **alien?**

A Mars-upial.

**A**

CUTLERY 1:
Have a knife day!

CUTLERY 2:
See you spoon!

**Q**

Where do giraffes take classes?

In high school.

**A**

KNOCK,
KNOCK.

*Who's there?*
Brew.
*Brew who?*
I'm so glad to
see brew!

People have been
raising chickens for
more than 7,000 years.

181

Fisher cats are only found in North America. They are closely related to badgers, mink, and otters.

KNOCK, KNOCK.

*Who's there?*
Sumatra.
*Sumatra who?*
What's Sumatra with you?

**Q** Where do fish professors teach?

**A** Tunaversity.

**Q** Why is a porcupine so good at volleyball?

**A** Because it can really spike the ball.

**Q** How do pandas block their doors?

**A** With a bearricade.

**Q** What's the difference between bird flu and swine flu?

**A** One requires tweetment and the other needs oinkment.

**BOY WITH POISON IVY:** I'm afraid I have to scratch our dinner plans.

**FRIEND:** Don't do anything rash; we can always reschedule.

The giant panda's diet is made up almost entirely of bamboo.

## TV shows for snack foods:

- *Spongecake SquarePants*
- *What Not to Share*
- *Sesame Seed Street*
- *The Walking Bread*
- *Bill Rye the Science Guy*
- *A Series of Unfortunate Eggvents*

KNOCK, KNOCK.

Who's there?
Crumb.
*Crumb who?*
I'm hoping you'll crumb to your senses.

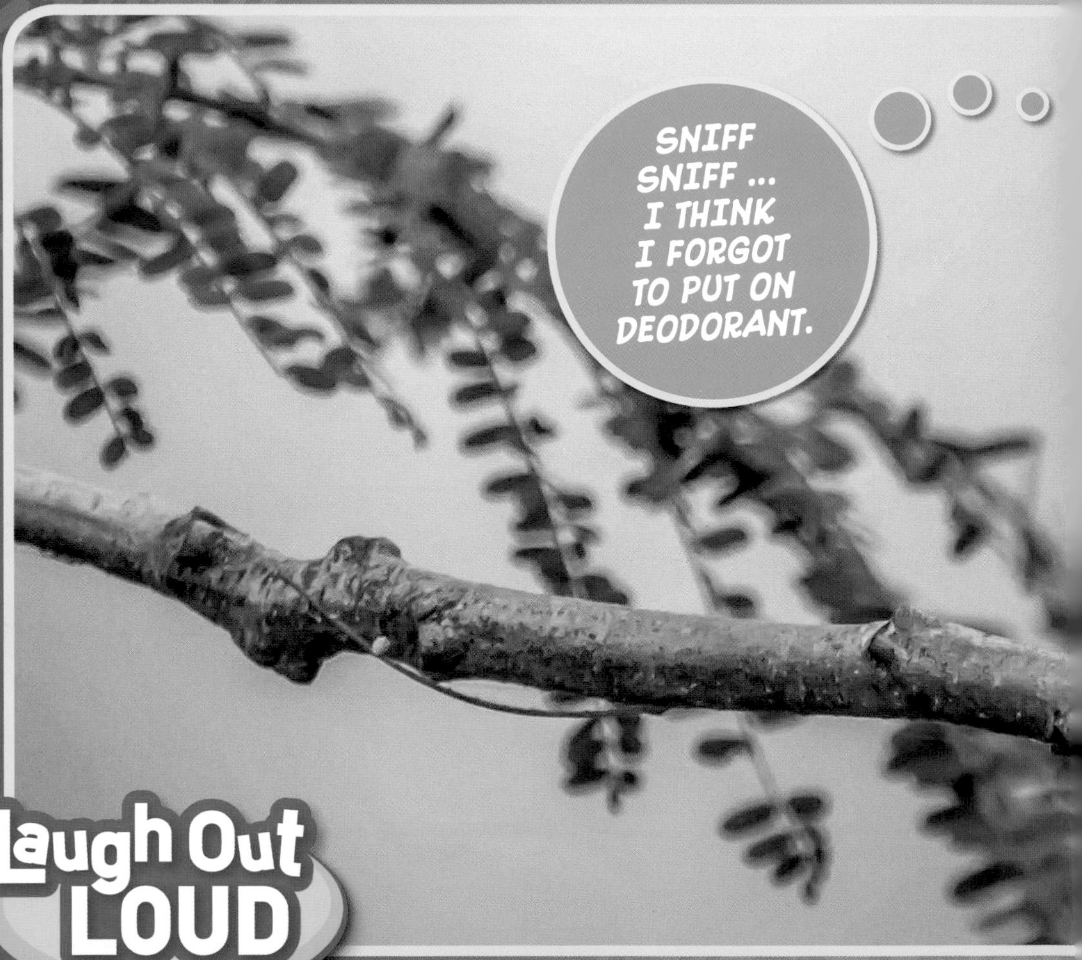


Laugh Out LOUD

KNOCK, KNOCK.

Who's there?
Frappé.
Frappé who?
Frappé birthday to you!

The bald eagle has been the national emblem of the United States since 1782.

**Q** Where does a rabbit go to get its fur done?

**A** The hare-dresser.

**Q** What happens when cattle get tired of standing?

**A** They cowlapse.

**TONGUE TWISTER!**

Say this fast three times:

I insist on **mitts during frosts** and **mists.**

191

Q What does an aardvark take when it has heartburn?

A Ant-acid.

I LOVE YOGA! AND NOT JUST DOWNWARD DOG!

Laugh Out LOUD

Q What do you call a deer that uses all of its hooves to draw?

A Bambi-dextrous.

Q Who do sea birds go to the movies with?

A Their gull friends.

River otters use their strong tails to help them steer while swimming underwater.

KNOCK, KNOCK.

Who's there?
Latte.
Latte who?
It's beginning to look a latte like Christmas.

A tiger's teeth are four inches (10 cm) long.

KNOCK, KNOCK.

*Who's there?*
Filter.
*Filter who?*
My mom filter pool, so we can go swimming!

The Javan gliding frog uses its large webbed feet to "fly" from tree to tree.

**KNOCK, KNOCK.**

*Who's there?*
Scone.
*Scone who?*
Come to the park. It's scone to be fun.

# Jobs for dogs:

- Barkeologist
- Lab technician
- Border collie guard
- Puppeteer
- Pawty planner

**DUCK:** Who's paying for dinner tonight?

**SKUNK:** I don't have a scent.

**DEER:** I don't have a buck to spare.

**DUCK:** I guess we'll just put it on my bill.

**Q** What do you call a grizzly with no socks on?

**A** Bearfoot.

**Q** What do you call the winner of an ape race?

**A** The chimpion.

Q

Why did the
**Dalmatian
refuse** to
bathe in
**dishwasher
detergent?**

A

He didn't want to
come out spotless.

Skunks will try to scare a predator by stomping their feet, slapping their tail on the ground, or even doing a handstand dance before spraying.

**KNOCK,**

**KNOCK.**

*Who's there?*
**Wheat.**
*Wheat who?*
**Wheat a second ...
this is the wrong
house!**

# JOKE**FINDER**

# JOKE**FINDER**

# ILLUSTRATION CREDITS

Since 1888, the National Geographic Society has funded more than 12,000 research, exploration, and preservation projects around the world. The Society receives funds from National Geographic Partners, LLC, funded in part by your purchase. A portion of the proceeds from this book supports this vital work. To learn more, visit natgeo.com/info.

For more information, visit nationalgeographic.com, call 1-800-647-5463, or write to the following address:

National Geographic Partners
1145 17th Street N.W.
Washington, D.C. 20036-4688 U.S.A.

Visit us online at nationalgeographic.com/books

For librarians and teachers: ngchildrensbooks.org

More for kids from National Geographic: natgeokids.com

*National Geographic Kids* magazine inspires children to explore their world with fun yet educational articles on animals, science, nature, and more. Using fresh storytelling and amazing photography, *Nat Geo Kids* shows kids ages 6 to 14 the fascinating truth about the world—and why they should care. **kids.nationalgeographic.com/subscribe**

For information about special discounts for bulk purchases, please contact National Geographic Books Special Sales: specialsales@natgeo.com

For rights or permissions inquiries, please contact National Geographic Books Subsidiary Rights: bookrights@natgeo.com

**Editorial, Design, and Production by Plan B Book Packagers**

The publisher would like to thank: Paige Towler, associate editor; Callie Broaddus, senior designer; Sarah J. Mock, senior photo editor; Molly Reid, production editor; and Gus Tello and Anne LeongSon, design production assistants.

Trade paperback ISBN 978-1-4263-3310-1
Reinforced library binding ISBN: 978-1-4263-3311-8

Printed in China
18/PPS/1